Learn to Make
Mile-A-Minute
Baby Afghans

Featuring speedy strips, these six wraps make precious gifts!

6

11

15

22

28

34

LEISURE ARTS, INC. • Maumelle, Arkansas

How is a Mile-A-Minute Pattern Created?

No matter what your skill level or the look you desire,
there is a Mile-A-Minute afghan just right for you.
Here's the three basic steps to a mile-a-minute pattern.

1. Make the center strip. Mile-a-minute afghans begin with a center strip, whether it is worked in rows *(4 rows shown in A)* or around a long beginning chain *(indicated by red line in B)*.

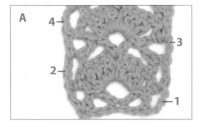

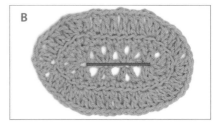

2. Work the border around the center strip. The border is added to the center strip and defines the final shape.

3. Join the completed strips. The instructions will tell which method to use to finish your afghan.

Many mile-a-minute afghans are created by making multiples of the same strip and whipstitching the strips together. Some patterns use a no-sew joining to join the strips like the Miles of Shells pattern on page 6 or the Easter Mile-A-Minute pattern on page 11.

Try it Yourself!

Here is one example of a center strip worked in rows, then whipstitched together after the strips are completed. You will need some medium weight yarn, a size H (5 mm) hook, and a yarn needle. And if you use cotton yarn, this sample would work great as a mile-a-minute trivet.

STRIP (Make 2)
Ch 12.

Work Center Row 1 (Wrong side)**:** Dc in sixth ch from hook **(5 skipped chs count as first dc plus ch 2)**, skip next 2 chs, (dc, ch 4, dc) in next ch, skip next 2 chs, (dc, ch 2, dc) in last ch: 6 dc and 3 sps.

Note: Loop a short piece of yarn around the **back** of any stitch on Row 1 to mark **right** side and bottom edge.

Work Center Row 2: Ch 5 **(counts as first dc plus ch 2, now and throughout)**, turn; dc in next ch-2 sp, (4 dc, ch 1, 4 dc) in next ch-4 sp, (dc, ch 2, dc) in last ch-2 sp: 12 dc and 3 sps.

Work Center Row 3: Ch 5, turn; dc in next ch-2 sp, (dc, ch 4, dc) in next ch-1 sp, (dc, ch 2, dc) in last ch-2 sp: 6 dc and 3 sps.

Work Center Rows 4 and 5: Repeat Rows 2 and 3; do **not** finish off your yarn. Your Center Strip is now completed *(Fig. A)*.

Work Border: Ch 1, turn; (sc, hdc, dc) in first ch-2 sp, (3 dc, ch 3, 3 dc) in next ch-4 sp, (dc, hdc, sc) in last ch-2 sp, ch 1 (corner), 2 dc in same sp; working in ends of rows, (ch 1, 2 dc in next row) 4 times, ch 1 (corner), (sc, hdc, dc) in same row, skip next 3 chs, (3 dc, ch 3, 3 dc) in free loop of next ch *(Fig. 3, page 41)*, skip last 3 chs; working in ends of rows, (dc, hdc, sc) in first row, ch 1 (corner), 2 dc in same row, (ch 1, 2 dc in next row) 4 times, ch 1 (corner); join with slip st to first sc, finish off.

Here is one completed Strip *(Fig. B)*

Fig. A	Fig. B

 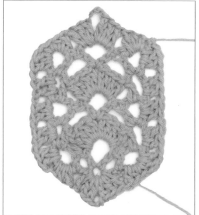

Now that you have completed both strips, you are ready to join them using whipstitch *(Fig. 6, page 42)*.

Joining: Place both strips with **wrong** sides together and bottom edges at the same end. Working through **both** loops of each st on **both** pieces, whipstitch strips together, beginning in first corner ch and ending in next corner ch.

Here is the completed Mile-A-Minute sampler *(Fig. C)*.

Fig. C

Congratulations!
See how easy that was?

Now choose one of the six wonderful Mile-A-Minute baby afghan patterns in this book and your favorite yarn and start crocheting — a mile a minute!

MILES OF SHELLS

 **EASY**

Finished Size: 38" x 50" (96.5 cm x 127 cm)

SHOPPING LIST

Yarn (Medium Weight)
[3.5 ounces, 170 yards
(100 grams, 156 meters) per skein]:
- ☐ Blue - 6 skeins
- ☐ White - 4 skeins
- ☐ Pink - 3 skeins

Crochet Hook
- ☐ Size G (4 mm) **or** size needed for gauge

GAUGE INFORMATION

Center of Strip = 2½" (6.25 cm) and 7 rows = 4" (10 cm)

Each Strip = 3¼" (8.25 cm) wide

Gauge Swatch: 2½"w x 4"h (6.25 cm x 10 cm)

Work same as Rows 1-7 of Center: 6 dc and 3 sps.

—— STITCH GUIDE ——

TREBLE CROCHET
(abbreviated tr)

YO twice, insert hook in st or sp indicated, YO and pull up a loop (4 loops on hook), (YO and draw through 2 loops on hook) 3 times.

DOUBLE TREBLE CROCHET
(abbreviated dtr)

YO 3 times, insert hook in st or sp indicated, YO and pull up a loop (5 loops on hook), (YO and draw through 2 loops on hook) 4 times.

INSTRUCTIONS
Strip (Make 10)
CENTER

With Blue, ch 12.

Row 1 (Wrong side)**:** Dc in sixth ch from hook, skip next 2 chs, (dc, ch 4, dc) in next ch, skip next 2 chs, (dc, ch 2, dc) in last ch: 5 dc and 3 sps.

Note: Loop a short piece of yarn around back of any stitch on Row 1 to mark **right** side and bottom edge.

Row 2: Ch 5 (**counts as first dc plus ch 2, now and throughout**), turn; dc in next ch-2 sp, (4 dc, ch 1, 4 dc) in next ch-4 sp, (dc, ch 2, dc) in last sp: 12 dc and 3 sps.

Row 3: Ch 5, turn; dc in next ch-2 sp, (dc, ch 4, dc) in next ch-1 sp, (dc, ch 2, dc) in last ch-2 sp: 6 dc and 3 sps.

Rows 4-81: Repeat Rows 2 and 3, 39 times changing to White in last dc on Row 81 *(Fig. 4, page 42)*.

EDGING

Ch 1, turn; (sc, hdc, dc) in first ch-2 sp, (3 tr, dtr, 3 tr) in next ch-4 sp, (dc, hdc, sc) in last ch-2 sp, ch 1 (corner), 2 dc in same sp, ch 1, (2 dc in end of next row, ch 1) across to last sp, 2 dc in last sp, ch 1 (corner), (sc, hdc, dc) in same sp, skip next sp, (3 tr, dtr, 3 tr) in free loop of next ch *(Fig. 3, page 41)*, skip next sp, (dc, hdc, sc) in last sp, ch 1 (corner), 2 dc in same sp, (ch 1, 2 dc in end of next row) across, ch 1 (corner); join with slip st to first sc, finish off.

Assembly

Join 2 Strips as follows: With **wrong** sides together and having top of Strips to the **right**, join Pink with slip st in first corner ch-1 sp on **first Strip**; ch 1, sc in same sp, ch 2, sc in first corner ch-1 sp on **second Strip** *(Fig. 5, page 42)*, ch 2, ★ skip next st on **first Strip**, sc in next st, ch 2, skip next st on **second Strip**, sc in next st, ch 2; repeat from ★ across to within 2 dc of next corner ch-1 sp on **both** Strips, skip next 2 dc on **first Strip**, sc in next corner ch-1 sp, ch 2, skip next 2 dc on **second Strip**, sc in next corner ch-1 sp; finish off.

Join remaining Strips in the same manner.

Trim

Rnd 1: With **right** side facing and bottom edge toward you, join Pink with slip st in top right corner ch-1 sp; ch 1, (sc, ch 1, sc) in same sp, † sc in next 6 sts, (sc, ch 1, sc) in next dtr, sc in next 6 sts, ★ 3 sc in next joining, sc in next 6 sts, (sc, ch 1, sc) in next dtr, sc in next 6 sts; repeat from ★ 8 times **more**, (sc, ch 1, sc) in next corner ch-1 sp, sc in next dc, (ch 1, skip next st, sc in next st) across to within one dc of next corner ch-1 sp, ch 1, skip next dc †, (sc, ch 1, sc) in corner ch-1 sp, repeat from † to † once; join with slip st to first sc: 584 sc.

Rnd 2: Slip st in first corner ch-1 sp, ch 1, (sc, ch 2) twice in same sp, † skip next 2 sc, sc in next sc, (ch 2, skip next sc, sc in next sc) twice, ch 2, skip next sc, (sc, ch 2) twice in next ch-1 sp, ★ skip next sc, sc in next sc, (ch 2, skip next sc, sc in next sc) 7 times, ch 2, skip next sc, (sc, ch 2) twice in next ch-1 sp; repeat from ★ 8 times **more**, skip next sc, sc in next sc, (ch 2, skip next sc, sc in next sc) twice, ch 2, skip next 2 sc, (sc, ch 2) twice in next corner ch-1 sp, (sc in next ch-1 sp, ch 2) across to next corner ch-1 sp †, (sc, ch 2) twice in corner ch-1 sp, repeat from † to † once; join with slip st to first sc, finish off.

Design by Carole Prior.

EASTER MILE-A-MINUTE

 **EASY +**

Shown on page 13.
Finished Size: 39" x 48" (99 cm x 122 cm)

SHOPPING LIST

Yarn (Light Weight) **3** LIGHT
[5 ounces, 362 yards
(140 grams, 331 meters) per skein]:
☐ Lavender - 2 skeins
☐ Green - 2 skeins
☐ Yellow - 1 skein

Crochet Hook
☐ Size H (5 mm) **or** size needed for gauge

Additional Supplies
☐ Yarn needle

GAUGE INFORMATION

16 dc and 8 rows = 4" (10 cm)
  Each Strip = 4¼" (10.75 cm)
  wide
Gauge Swatch: 4" (10 cm)
  square
With Green, ch 18.
Row 1: Dc in fourth ch from hook
and in each ch across: 16 sts.
Rows 4-8: Ch 3 **(counts as first
dc)**, turn; dc in next dc and in
each st across.
Finish off.

INSTRUCTIONS
First Strip

With Green, ch 166.

Rnd 1 (Right side)**:** Dc in fourth ch
from hook **(3 skipped chs count
as first dc)**, ch 1, (dc in same ch,
ch 1) twice, 2 dc in same ch, **[**skip
next 2 chs, (dc, ch 1, dc) in next
ch**]** across to last 3 chs, skip next
2 chs, in last ch work **[**2 dc, ch 1,
(dc, ch 1) twice, 2 dc**]**; working in
free loops of beginning ch *(Fig. 3,
page 41)*, skip next 2 chs, ★ (dc,
ch 1, dc) in next ch, skip next
2 chs; repeat from ★ across; join
with slip st to first dc: 224 dc and
112 ch-1 sps.

Note: Loop a short piece of
yarn around any stitch to mark
Rnd 1 as **right** side.

Rnd 2: Ch 1, sc in same st and
in each dc and each ch-1 sp
around; join with slip st to first
sc, finish off: 336 sc.

Rnd 3: With **right** side facing
and working in Back Loops
Only *(Fig. 1)*, join Lavender
with slip st in center sc on
either end; ch 3 **(counts as first
dc)**, dc in same st, ch 1, dc in
next 3 sc, ch 1, 3 dc in next sc,
ch 1, (dc in next 3 sc, ch 1) 53
times, 3 dc in next sc, ch 1, (dc
in next 3 sc, ch 1, 3 dc in next
sc, ch 1) twice, (dc in next 3 sc,
ch 1) across to last 4 sc, 3 dc
in next sc, ch 1, dc in last 3 sc,
ch 1, dc in same st as first dc;
join with slip st to first dc:
348 dc and 116 ch-1 sps.

Fig. 1

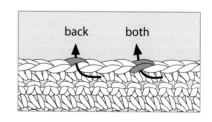

Rnd 4: Ch 2, working in both loops, 2 hdc in same st, slip st in next ch-1 sp, skip next dc, (3 hdc in next dc, slip st in next ch-1 sp, skip next dc) around; join with slip st to top of beginning ch-2, finish off: 464 sts.

Rnd 5: With **right** side facing and working in Back Loops Only, join Yellow with sc in second slip st to **right** of joining *(see Joining with Sc, page 41)*; (2 sc, ch 1, 3 sc) in same st, † ★ ch 4, slip st in last sc made, skip next 3 sts, (3 sc, ch 1, 3 sc) in next slip st; repeat from ★ 2 times **more**, ch 1, (skip next 3 hdc, 3 hdc in next slip st, ch 1) 54 times, skip next 3 hdc †, (3 sc, ch 1, 3 sc) in next slip st, repeat from † to † once; join with slip st to **both** loops of first sc, finish off.

Remaining 8 Strips

Work same as First Strip through Rnd 4: 464 sts.

Rnd 5 (Joining rnd)**:** With **right** side facing and working in Back Loops Only, join Yellow with sc in second slip st to **right** of joining; (2 sc, ch 1, 3 sc) in same st, † [ch 4, slip st in last sc made, skip next 3 sts, (3 sc, ch 1, 3 sc) in next slip st] 3 times, ch 1 †, (skip next 3 hdc, 3 hdc in next slip st, ch 1) 54 times, skip next 3 hdc, (3 sc, ch 1, 3 sc) in next slip st, repeat from † to † once, skip next 3 hdc, 3 hdc in next slip st, ch 1, holding Strips with **wrong** sides together, ★ slip st in corresponding ch-1 sp on **previous Strip** *(Fig. 5, page 42)*, ch 1, skip next 3 hdc on **new Strip**, 3 hdc in next slip st, ch 1; repeat from ★ across; join with slip st to **both** loops of first sc, finish off.

Design by Jennine DeMoss.

PINEAPPLE PARADE

 **INTERMEDIATE**

Shown on page 17.
Finished Size: 36" x 46" (91.5 cm x 117 cm)

SHOPPING LIST

Yarn (Light Weight) **LIGHT 3**
[5 ounces, 388 yards
(140 grams, 355 meters) per skein]:
☐ Pink - 5 skeins
☐ Blue - 3 skeins

Crochet Hook
☐ Size F (3.75 mm) **or** size needed for gauge

Additional Supplies
☐ Yarn needle

GAUGE INFORMATION

Rows 3-14 = 5½" (14 cm)
Each Strip = 5¼" (13.25 cm)
at widest point

Gauge Swatch: 4¼"w x 3¾"h
(10.75 cm x 9.5 cm)
Work same as Strip A, page 26,
through Row 7: 9 ch-2 sps.

muestra
CHAIN
Cadena
SPACE

dc - doble crochet
st - STITCH

— STITCH GUIDE —

BEGINNING SHELL (uses one sp) *space*
Turn; skip first dc, slip st in next
dc and in next ch-2 sp, ch 3, (dc,
ch 2, 2 dc) in same sp.

SHELL (uses one sp)
(2 Dc, ch 2, 2 dc) in sp indicated.

SCALLOP
(Slip st, ch 2, hdc) in st indicated.

DECREASE (uses next 2 dc)
YO, insert hook in same st as
joining on same strip, YO and
pull up a loop, YO and draw
through 2 loops on hook, YO,
skip next joining, insert hook in
same st as joining on next strip,
YO and pull up a loop, YO and
draw through 2 loops on hook,
YO and draw through all 3 loops
on hook.

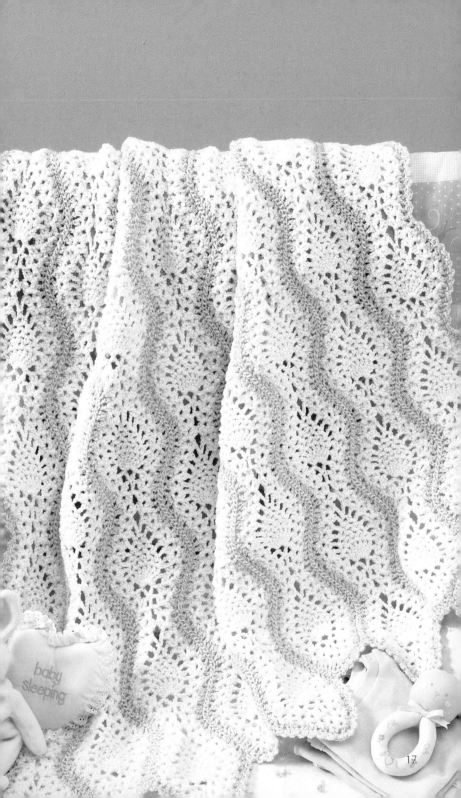

INSTRUCTIONS
Strip A (Make 5)

With Pink, ch 4; join with slip st to form a ring.

Row 1: Ch 3 (**counts as first dc, now and throughout**), dc in ring, (ch 2, 2 dc in ring) twice: 6 dc and 2 ch-2 sps.

Row 2 (Right side)**:** Work Beginning Shell, ch 1, work Shell in last ch-2 sp: 8 dc and 3 sps.

Note: Loop a short piece of yarn around any stitch to mark Row 2 as **right** side and bottom edge.

Row 3: Work Beginning Shell, ch 1, dc in next ch-1 sp, ch 1, work Shell in last ch-2 sp: 9 dc and 4 sps.

Row 4: Work Beginning Shell, ch 1, skip next ch-1 sp, (dc, ch 3, dc) in next dc, ch 1, skip next ch-1 sp, work Shell in last ch-2 sp: 10 dc and 5 sps.

Row 5: Work Beginning Shell, ch 1, skip next ch-1 sp, 7 dc in next ch-3 sp, ch 1, skip next ch-1 sp, work Shell in last ch-2 sp: 15 dc and 4 sps.

Row 6: Work Beginning Shell, ch 1, skip next ch-1 sp, (hdc in next dc, ch 1) 7 times, skip next ch-1 sp, work Shell in last ch-2 sp: 10 sps.

Row 7: Work Beginning Shell, ch 2, skip next ch-1 sp, (sc in next ch-1 sp, ch 2) 6 times, skip next ch-1 sp, work Shell in last ch-2 sp: 9 ch-2 sps.

Row 8: Work Beginning Shell, ch 2, skip next ch-2 sp, (sc in next ch-2 sp, ch 2) 5 times, skip next ch-2 sp, work Shell in last ch-2 sp: 8 ch-2 sps.

Row 9: Work Beginning Shell, ch 2, skip next ch-2 sp, (sc in next ch-2 sp, ch 2) 4 times, skip next ch-2 sp, work Shell in last ch-2 sp: 7 ch-2 sps.

Row 10: Work Beginning Shell, ch 2, skip next ch-2 sp, (sc in next ch-2 sp, ch 2) 3 times, skip next ch-2 sp, work Shell in last ch-2 sp: 6 ch-2 sps.

Row 11: Work Beginning Shell, ch 2, skip next ch-2 sp, (sc in next ch-2 sp, ch 2) twice, skip next ch-2 sp, work Shell in last ch-2 sp: 5 ch-2 sps.

Row 12: Work Beginning Shell, ch 2, skip next ch-2 sp, sc in next ch-2 sp, ch 2, skip next ch-2 sp, work Shell in last ch-2 sp: 4 ch-2 sps.

Row 13: Work Beginning Shell, skip next 2 ch-2 sps, work Shell in last ch-2 sp: 8 dc and 2 ch-2 sps.

Row 14: Work Beginning Shell, ch 1, work Shell in last ch-2 sp: 3 sps.

Rows 15-96: Repeat Rows 3-14, 6 times; then repeat Rows 3-12 once **more**: 4 ch-2 sps.

Row 97: Turn; skip first dc, slip st in next dc and in next ch-2 sp, ch 3, (dc, ch 1, 2 dc) in same sp, skip next 2 ch-2 sps, (2 dc, ch 1, 2 dc) in last ch-2 sp: 2 ch-1 sps.

Row 98: Turn; skip first dc, slip st in next dc and in next ch-1 sp, ch 3, YO, insert hook in same sp, YO and pull up a loop, YO and draw through 2 loops on hook, YO, insert hook in next ch-1 sp, YO and pull up a loop, YO and draw through 2 loops on hook, YO and draw through all 3 loops on hook, dc in same sp; finish off: 3 sts.

BORDER

With **right** side facing, join Variegated with dc in beginning ring *(see Joining With Dc, page 41)*; (ch 1, dc) twice in same sp; working around dc at end of rows, (dc, ch 1, dc) in first row, 2 dc in each of next 4 rows, ♥ (dc, ch 1, dc) in next 2 rows, place marker around last dc made for joining and st placement, ch 1, dc in same row, ★ † (dc, ch 1, dc) in next row, 2 dc in each of next 3 rows, dc in next 3 rows, 2 dc in each of next 3 rows †, (dc, ch 1, dc) in next row, dc in next row, (ch 1, dc in same row) twice; repeat from ★ 5 times **more**, then repeat from † to † once, (dc, ch 1, dc) in each of next 2 rows, place marker around last dc made for joining and st placement, ch 1, dc in same row, (dc, ch 1, dc) in next row ♥, 2 dc in each of next 5 rows, (dc, ch 1, dc) in last row, skip first dc on Row 98, dc in next st, (ch 1, dc in same st) twice; working around dc at end of rows, (dc, ch 1, dc) in same row, 2 dc in each of next 5 rows, repeat from ♥ to ♥ once, 2 dc in each of next 4 rows, (dc, ch 1, dc) in last row; join with slip st to first dc, finish off.

Strip B (Make 4)

Work same as Strip A through Row 84: 4 ch-2 sps.

Rows 85 and 86: Work same as Rows 97 and 98 of Strip A: 3 sts.

BORDER

With **right** side facing, join Variegated with dc in beginning ring; (ch 1, dc) twice in same sp; working around dc at end of rows, (dc, ch 1, dc) in first row, † dc in next row, place marker around dc just made for joining and st placement, dc in same row, 2 dc in each of next 3 rows, (dc, ch 1, dc) in next row, dc in next row, (ch 1, dc in same row) twice, (dc, ch 1, dc) in next row, ★ 2 dc in each of next 3 rows, dc in next 3 rows, 2 dc in each of next 3 rows, (dc, ch 1, dc) in next row, dc in next row, (ch 1, dc in same row) twice, (dc, ch 1, dc) in next row; repeat from ★ 5 times **more**, 2 dc in each of next 4 rows, place marker around last dc made for joining and st placement †, 2 dc in next row, (dc, ch 1, dc) in last row, skip first dc on Row 86, dc in next st, (ch 1, dc in same st) twice; working around dc at end of rows, (dc, ch 1, dc) in same row, 2 dc in next row, repeat from † to † once, (dc, ch 1, dc) in last row; join with slip st to first dc, finish off.

Assembly

Afghan is assembled by joining Strips in the following order: Strip A, (Strip B, Strip A) 4 times.

Join Strips as follows:
With Variegated, having bottom edges at same end and working through **both** loops of each st on **both** pieces, whipstitch Strips together *(Fig. 6, page 42)*, beginning in first marked dc and ending in next marked dc.

EDGING

Remove 2 markers from unjoined edge of each outer Strip A (4 markers total). When working Edging, dc and chs count as sts.

With **right** side of top edge facing, join Variegated with slip st in ch before center dc at top point on first Strip A; ch 2, hdc in same st, ★ † (skip next st, work Scallop in next st) across to within 3 sts of next joined dc, skip next dc, slip st in next dc, skip next st, decrease; repeat from ★ 7 times **more**, skip next ch †, (work Scallop in next st, skip next st) 26 times, slip st in next 2 dc, [(work Scallop in next st, skip next st) 12 times, slip st in next 2 dc] 6 times, work Scallop in next dc, repeat from † to † once, (work Scallop in next st, skip next st) 24 times, slip st in next 2 dc, [(work Scallop in next st, skip next st) 12 times, slip st in next 2 dc] 6 times, (work Scallop in next st, skip next st) across; join with slip st to first slip st, finish off.

Design by Anne Halliday.

WAVY STRIPS

Finished Size: 38½" x 51¼" (98 cm x 130 cm)

SHOPPING LIST

Yarn (Light Weight)
[7 ounces, 575 yards
(198 grams, 525 meters) per skein]:
- ☐ Green - 2 skeins
- ☐ Lavender - 2 skeins
- ☐ White - 1 skein

Crochet Hook
- ☐ Size G (4 mm) **or** size needed for gauge

Additional Supplies
- ☐ Yarn needle

GAUGE INFORMATION

2 repeats (40 sts) = 10¼" (26 cm)
Gauge Swatch: 10¼" x 3"
   (26 cm x 7.5 cm)
With Green, ch 42.
Work same as Strip A.

Each row is worked across length of Strip. When joining yarn and finishing off, leave a 6" (15 cm) length to be worked into fringe.

— STITCH GUIDE —

TREBLE CROCHET
   (abbreviated tr)
YO twice, insert hook in st or sp indicated, YO and pull up a loop (4 loops on hook), (YO and draw through 2 loops on hook) 3 times.

CLUSTER
Ch 4, sc in second ch from hook, 2 dc in next ch, sc in last ch (4-st row made); fold row in half from **right** to **left**, slip st in skipped ch at edge of first sc made.

INSTRUCTIONS
Strip A (Make 9)
FIRST HALF
With Green, ch 202.

Row 1 (Right side)**:** Sc in second ch from hook, ch 1, skip next ch, sc in next ch, ★ † ch 1, skip next ch, hdc in next ch, ch 1, skip next ch, dc in next ch, ch 1, skip next ch, tr in next ch, ch 1, skip next ch, (tr, ch 1) twice in next ch, skip next ch, tr in next ch, ch 1, skip next ch, dc in next ch, ch 1, skip next ch, hdc in next ch, ch 1, skip next ch, sc in next ch †, (work Cluster, skip next ch, sc in next ch) twice; repeat from ★ 8 times **more**, then repeat from † to † once, ch 1, skip next ch, sc in last ch: 31 sc, 20 hdc, 20 dc, 40 tr, 18 Clusters, and 92 chs.

Note: Loop a short piece of yarn around last sc made to mark **right** side and top edge.

Row 2: Ch 1, turn; keeping Clusters to **right** side, sc in first sc, (ch 1, skip next ch, sc in next st) 5 times, ch 1, sc in next ch, ch 1, sc in next tr, ★ (ch 1, skip next ch or Cluster, sc in next st) 10 times, ch 1, sc in next ch, ch 1, sc in next tr; repeat from ★ across to last 10 sts, (ch 1, skip next ch, sc in next st) 5 times; finish off: 121 sc and 120 chs.

Row 3: With **right** side facing, join White with sc in first sc *(see Joining With Sc, page 41)*; ★ ch 1, skip next ch, sc in next sc; repeat from ★ across; finish off.

SECOND HALF

Row 1: With **right** side of First Half facing and working in free loops of beginning ch *(Fig. 3, page 41)*, join Green with sc in first ch; ch 1, skip next ch, sc in next ch, ★ † ch 1, skip next ch, hdc in next ch, ch 1, skip next ch, dc in next ch, ch 1, skip next ch, tr in next ch, ch 1, skip next ch, (tr, ch 1) twice in next ch, skip next ch, tr in next ch, ch 1, skip next ch, dc in next ch, ch 1, skip next ch, hdc in next ch, ch 1, skip next ch, sc in next ch †, (work Cluster, skip next ch, sc in next ch) twice; repeat from ★ 8 times **more**, then repeat from † to † once, ch 1, skip next ch, sc in last ch: 31 sc, 20 hdc, 20 dc, 40 tr, 18 Clusters, and 92 chs.

Rows 2 and 3: Work same as First Half of Strip A.

Strip B (Make 8)
FIRST HALF

With Lavender, ch 205.

Row 1 (Right side): Tr in fifth ch from hook (**4 skipped chs count as first tr**), ch 1, ★ † skip next ch, tr in next ch, ch 1, skip next ch, dc in next ch, ch 1, skip next ch, hdc in next ch, ch 1, skip next ch, sc in next ch, (work Cluster, skip next ch, sc in next ch) twice, ch 1, skip next ch, hdc in next ch, ch 1, skip next ch, dc in next ch, ch 1, skip next ch, tr in next ch, ch 1, skip next ch †, (tr, ch 1) twice in next ch; repeat from ★ 8 times **more**, then repeat from † to † once, 2 tr in last ch: 30 sc, 20 hdc, 20 dc, 42 tr, 20 Clusters, and 89 chs.

Note: Mark last tr made as **right** side and top edge.

Row 2: Ch 1, turn; keeping Clusters to **right** side, sc in first tr, ch 1, sc in next tr, (ch 1, skip next ch or Cluster, sc in next st) 10 times, ★ ch 1, sc in next ch, ch 1, sc in next tr, (ch 1, skip next ch or Cluster, sc in next st) 10 times; repeat from ★ across to last tr, ch 1, sc in last tr; finish off: 121 sc and 120 chs.

Row 3: With **right** side facing, join White with sc in first sc; ★ ch 1, skip next ch, sc in next sc; repeat from ★ across; finish off.

SECOND HALF

Row 1: With **right** side facing and working in free loops of beginning ch, join Lavender with slip st in first ch; ch 4 (**counts as first tr**), tr in same ch as joining, ch 1, ★ † skip next ch, tr in next ch, ch 1, skip next ch, dc in next ch, ch 1, skip next ch, hdc in next ch, ch 1, skip next ch, sc in next ch, (work Cluster, skip next ch, sc in next ch) twice, ch 1, skip next ch, hdc in next ch, ch 1, skip next ch, dc in next ch, ch 1, skip next ch, tr in next ch, ch 1, skip next ch †, (tr, ch 1) twice in next ch; repeat from ★ 8 times **more**, then repeat from † to † once, 2 tr in next ch: 30 sc, 20 hdc, 20 dc, 42 tr, 20 Clusters, and 89 chs.

Rows 2 and 3: Work same as First Half of Strip B.

Assembly

Afghan is assembled by joining Strips in the following order: Strip A, (Strip B, Strip A) 8 times.

Join Strips as follows: With White, having top edges at same end and working through **both** loops of each st on **both** pieces, whipstitch Strips together *(Fig. 6, page 42)* across long edge.

EDGING

With **right** side of long edge facing, join White with slip st in first sc on Row 3; (slip st in next ch-1 sp, ch 1) across to last sc, slip st in last sc; finish off.

Repeat across opposite long edge.

Holding 2 strands of corresponding color yarn together, each 24" (61 cm) long, add additional fringe evenly across short edges of Afghan *(Figs. 7a & b, page 43)*.

Design by Anne Halliday.

LEMON DROP

 **INTERMEDIATE**

Finished Size: 39" x 51" (99 cm x 129.5 cm)

SHOPPING LIST

Yarn (Medium Weight) 🧶4
[5 ounces, 256 yards
(142 grams, 234 meters) per skein]:
- ☐ White - 5 skeins
- ☐ Yellow - 4 skeins

Crochet Hook
- ☐ Size I (5.5 mm) **or** size needed for gauge

Additional Supplies
- ☐ Yarn needle

GAUGE INFORMATION

Each Strip = 4" (10 cm) wide

Gauge Swatch: 3"w x 7"h (7.5 cm x 17.75 cm)

Foundation: With White, ch 3, dc in third ch from hook, ch 14, dc in third ch from hook: 2 rings.

Rnd 1 (Right side)**:** Ch 5, working across dc side of rings, (tr, ch 1) 6 times in first ring, † skip next 3 chs, sc in next ch, ch 1, (skip next ch, sc in next ch, ch 1) twice †, (tr, ch 1) 12 times in last ring; working in free loops of Foundation chs *(Fig. 3, page 41)* and across ch-3 side of rings, repeat from † to † once, (tr, ch 1) 5 times in same ring as beginning ch-5; join with slip st to fourth ch of beginning ch-5: 30 sts and 30 ch-1 sps.

Rnd 2: Ch 1, turn; sc in same st, ch 1, skip next ch, ★ sc in next st, ch 1, skip next ch; repeat from ★ around; join with slip st to first sc, finish off.

——STITCH GUIDE——

TREBLE CROCHET *(abbreviated tr)*

YO twice, insert hook in sp indicated, YO and pull up a loop (4 loops on hook), (YO and draw through 2 loops on hook) 3 times.

DECREASE (uses next 3 dc)

YO, † insert hook in **next** dc, YO and pull up a loop, YO and draw through 2 loops on hook †, YO, skip next dc, repeat from † to † once, YO and draw through all 3 loops on hook.

LEFT DECREASE

YO, insert hook in next dc, YO and pull up a loop, YO and draw through 2 loops on hook, skip next joining, ★ YO, insert hook in **next** dc, YO and pull up a loop, YO and draw through 2 loops on hook; repeat from ★ once **more**, YO and draw through all 4 loops on hook.

RIGHT DECREASE

★ YO, insert hook in **next** dc, YO and pull up a loop, YO and draw through 2 loops on hook; repeat from ★ once **more**, YO, skip next joining, insert hook in next dc, YO and pull up a loop, YO and draw through 2 loops on hook, YO and draw through all 4 loops on hook.

INSTRUCTIONS
Strip A (Make 6)

Foundation: With White, ch 3, dc in third ch from hook, (ch 14, dc in third ch from hook) 12 times: 13 rings.

Rnd 1 (Right side): Ch 5, working across dc side of rings, (tr, ch 1) 6 times in first ring, † skip next 3 chs, sc in next ch, ch 1, (skip next ch, sc in next ch, ch 1) twice, [(tr, ch 1) 5 times in next ring, skip next 3 chs, sc in next ch, ch 1, (skip next ch, sc in next ch, ch 1) twice] 11 times †, (tr, ch 1) 12 times in last ring; working in free loops of Foundation chs (*Fig. 3, page 41*) and across ch-3 side of rings, repeat from † to † once, (tr, ch 1) 5 times in same ring as beginning ch-5; join with slip st to fourth ch of beginning ch-5: 206 sts and 206 ch-1 sps.

Note: Loop a short piece of yarn around any stitch to mark Rnd 1 as **right** side.

Rnd 2: Ch 1, turn; sc in same st, ch 1, skip next ch, ★ sc in next st, ch 1, skip next ch; repeat from ★ around; join with slip st to first sc, finish off.

Rnd 3: With **right** side facing, join Yellow with slip st in same st as joining; ch 4 (**counts as first dc plus ch 1, now and throughout**), dc in same st, (ch 1, dc) twice in each of next 4 sc, † place marker around last ch-1 made for joining placement, ch 1, (dc in next sc, ch 1) twice, dc in next 3 sc, (ch 1, dc in next sc) twice, [(ch 1, dc) twice in next sc, ch 1, (dc in next sc, ch 1) twice, dc in next 3 sc, (ch 1, dc in next sc) twice] 11 times, (ch 1, dc) twice in next sc, place marker around last ch-1 made for joining placement †, (ch 1, dc) twice in each of next 7 sc, repeat from † to † once, ch 1, (dc, ch 1) twice in each of last 2 sc; join with slip st to first dc, finish off: 244 dc and 196 ch-1 sps.

Strip B (Make 5)

Foundation: With White, ch 3, dc in third ch from hook, (ch 14, dc in third ch from hook) 11 times: 12 rings.

Rnd 1 (Right side)**:** Ch 5, working across dc side of rings, (tr, ch 1) 6 times in first ring, † skip next 3 chs, sc in next ch, ch 1, (skip next ch, sc in next ch, ch 1) twice, [(tr, ch 1) 5 times in next ring, skip next 3 chs, sc in next ch, ch 1, (skip next ch, sc in next ch, ch 1) twice] 10 times †, (tr, ch 1) 12 times in last ring; working in free loops of Foundation chs and across ch-3 side of rings, repeat from † to † once, (tr, ch 1) 5 times in same ring as beginning ch-5; join with slip st to fourth ch of beginning ch-5: 190 sts and 190 ch-1 sps.

Note: Mark Rnd 1 as **right** side.

Rnd 2: Ch 1, turn; sc in same st, ch 1, skip next ch, ★ sc in next st, ch 1, skip next ch; repeat from ★ around; join with slip st to first sc, finish off.

Rnd 3: With **right** side facing, join Yellow with slip st in same st as joining; ch 4, dc in same st, (ch 1, dc) twice in each of next 2 sc, place marker around last ch-1 made for joining placement, † (ch 1, dc) twice in each of next 2 sc, ch 1, (dc in next sc, ch 1) twice, dc in next 3 sc, (ch 1, dc in next sc) twice, [(ch 1, dc) twice in next sc, ch 1, (dc in next sc, ch 1) twice, dc in next 3 sc, (ch 1, dc in next sc) twice] 10 times †, [(ch 1, dc)twice in each of next 3 sc, place marker around last ch-1 made for joining placement] twice, repeat from † to † once, (ch 1, dc) twice in each of next 3 sc, place marker around last ch-1 made for joining placement, ch 1; join with slip st to first dc, finish off: 226 dc and 182 ch-1 sps.

Assembly

With Yellow and working through **both** loops of each stitch on **both** pieces, whipstitch long edges of Strips together *(Fig. 6, page 42)*, beginning in first marked ch-1 and ending in next marked ch-1 in the following sequence: Strip A, (Strip B, Strip A) 5 times. Leave markers in place on outer Strips.

EDGING

Rnd 1: With **right** side facing, join Yellow with slip st in marked ch-1 sp at top right corner; ch 4, dc in next dc, (ch 1, dc in next dc) 12 times, † work left decrease, dc in next dc, ch 1, dc in next ch-1 sp, ch 1, dc in next dc, work right decrease, [dc in next dc, (ch 1, dc in next dc) 11 times, work left decrease, dc in next dc, ch 1, dc in next ch-1 sp, ch 1, dc in next dc, work right decrease] 4 times, (dc in next dc, ch 1) 13 times, [dc in next ch-1 sp, (ch 1, dc in next dc) 3 times, decrease, (dc in next dc, ch 1) 3 times] 12 times †, dc in next ch-1 sp, (ch 1, dc in next dc) 13 times, repeat from † to † once; join with slip st to first dc: 392 sts and 304 ch-1 sps.

Rnd 2: Slip st in next ch-1 sp, (ch 2, slip st in next ch-1 sp) 12 times, † skip next dc, slip st in next st, skip next dc, slip st in next ch-1 sp, ch 2, slip st in next ch-1 sp, skip next dc, slip st in next st, skip next dc, slip st in next ch-1 sp, [(ch 2, slip st in next ch-1 sp) 10 times, skip next dc, slip st in next st, skip next dc, slip st in next ch-1 sp, ch 2, slip st in next ch-1 sp, skip next dc, slip st in next st, skip next dc, slip st in next ch-1 sp] 4 times, (ch 2, slip st in next ch-1 sp) 15 times, skip next dc, slip st in next st, skip next dc, slip st in next ch-1 sp, [(ch 2, slip st in next ch-1 sp) 5 times, skip next dc, slip st in next st, skip next dc, slip st in next ch-1 sp] 11 times †, (ch 2, slip st in next ch-1 sp) 15 times, repeat from † to † once, ch 2, (slip st in next ch-1 sp, ch 2) twice; join with slip st to first slip st, finish off.

Design by Anne Halliday.

DAISIES FOR BABY

◀■■■▭ **INTERMEDIATE**

Finished Size: 30" x 44" (76 cm x 112 cm)

SHOPPING LIST

Yarn (Light Weight)
[5 ounces, 362 yards
(140 grams, 331 meters) per skein]:
- ☐ White - 3 skeins
- ☐ Yellow - 2 skeins
- ☐ Green - 1 skein

Crochet Hook
- ☐ Size H (5 mm) **or** size needed for gauge

GAUGE INFORMATION

16 dc = 4" (10 cm)
   Each Strip = 5" (12.75 cm) wide

Gauge Swatch: 4" (10 cm)
   square
With Green, ch 18.

Row 1: Dc in fourth ch from
hook (**3 skipped chs count as
first dc**) and in each ch across:
16 dc.

Rows 4-8: Ch 3 (**counts as first
dc**), turn; dc in next dc and in
each dc across.
Finish off.

——STITCH GUIDE——

CLUSTER (uses one st or sp)
★ YO twice, insert hook in st
or sp indicated, YO and pull up
a loop, (YO and draw through
2 loops on hook) twice; repeat
from ★ 2 times **more**, YO and
draw through all 4 loops on
hook.

INSTRUCTIONS
First Strip

With Green, ch 177.

Foundation (Right side)**:** Sc in
second ch from hook and in
each ch across; finish off: 176 sc.

Note: Loop a short piece of yarn
around any stitch to mark Row 1
as **right** side.

Rnd 1 (Daisy)**:** With **right** side
facing, join Yellow with slip st in
first sc; ch 3, ★ YO twice, insert
hook in same st, YO and pull up
a loop, (YO and draw through
2 loops on hook) twice; repeat
from ★ once **more**, YO and draw
through all 3 loops on hook
(**beginning Cluster made**), (ch 3,
work Cluster in same st) 5 times,
skip next 6 sc, [work Cluster in
next sc, (ch 3, work Cluster in
same st) twice, skip next 6 sc]
across to last sc, work Cluster

in last sc, (ch 3, work Cluster in same st) 5 times; working in each sp formed by Cluster groups, [work Cluster in next sp *(Fig. 2)*, (ch 3, work Cluster in same sp) twice] across; join with slip st to top of beginning Cluster, finish off: 26 Daisies.

Rnd 2: With **right** side facing, join White with slip st in second ch-3 sp; ch 3, 4 dc in same sp, 6 dc in next ch-3 sp, 5 dc in each of next 2 ch-3 sps, 3 dc in each of next 48 ch-3 sps, 5 dc in each of next 2 ch-3 sps, 6 dc in next ch-3 sp, 5 dc in each of next 2 ch-3 sps, 3 dc in each ch-3 sp across to last ch-3 sp, 5 dc in last ch-3 sp; join with slip st to top of beginning ch-3: 340 sts.

Rnd 3: Ch 1, sc in same st, ch 2, skip next dc, (sc in next dc, ch 2, skip next dc) around; join with slip st to first sc: 170 ch-2 sps.

Rnd 4: Slip st in first ch-2 sp, ch 3, 2 dc in same sp, 3 dc in each of next 7 ch-2 sps, 2 dc in each of next 77 ch-2 sps, 3 dc in each of next 8 ch-2 sps, 2 dc in each ch-2 sp across; join with slip st to top of beginning ch-3: 356 sts.

Rnd 5: Repeat Rnd 3; finish off: 178 ch-2 sps.

Rnd 6: With **right** side facing, join Green with slip st in last ch-2 sp; ch 1, sc in same sp, (ch 3, sc in next ch-2 sp) 89 times, place marker around last ch-3 made for joining placement, ch 3, (sc in next ch-2 sp, ch 3) around; join with slip st to first sc, finish off.

Next 4 Strips

Work same as First Strip through Rnd 5: 178 ch-2 sps.

Rnd 6 (Joining rnd): With **right** side facing, join Green with slip st in last ch-2 sp; ch 1, sc in same sp, (ch 3, sc in next ch-2 sp) 89 times, place marker around last ch-3 made for joining placement, (ch 3, sc in next ch-2 sp) 12 times, ch 2, holding **previous Strip** with **wrong** sides together, sc in marked ch-3 sp on **previous Strip** *(Fig. 5, page 42)*, ch 1, ★ sc in next ch-2 sp on **new Strip**, ch 2, sc in next ch-3 sp on **previous Strip**, ch 1; repeat from ★ across; join with slip st to first sc, finish off.

Last Strip

Work same as First Strip through Rnd 5: 178 ch-2 sps.

Rnd 6 (Joining rnd): With **right** side facing, join Green with slip st in last ch-2 sp; ch 1, sc in same sp, (ch 3, sc in next ch-2 sp) 101 times, ch 2, holding **previous Strip** with **wrong** sides together, sc in marked ch-3 sp on **previous Strip**, ch 1, ★ sc in next ch-2 sp on **new Strip**, ch 2, sc in next ch-3 sp on **previous Strip**, ch 1; repeat from ★ across; join with slip st to first sc, finish off.

Design by Terry Kimbrough.

GENERAL INSTRUCTIONS

ABBREVIATIONS

ch(s)   chain(s) *codena*
cm   centimeters
dc   double crochet(s)
dtr   double treble crochet(s) *pA first time*
hdc   half double crochet(s)
mm   millimeters
Rnd(s) Round(s)
sc   single crochet(s) *puntos bajo*
sp(s)   space(s)
st(s)   stitch(es) *punto*
tr   treble crochet(s) *p Alt 3*
YO   yarn over *hacer lazada*

SK = SKIP = puntos aers

stitch puntos

Hdc = punto alto

Knit = tejer

dcrease = desminui

increase = aumentar

SYMBOLS & TERMS

★ — work instructions following ★ as many **more** times as indicated in addition to the first time.

† to † or ♥ to ♥ — work all instructions from first † to second † or from first ♥ to second ♥ **as many** times as specified.

( ) or [ ] — work enclosed instructions **as many** times as specified by the number immediately following **or** work all enclosed instructions in the stitch or space indicated **or** contains explanatory remarks.

colon (:) — the number(s) given after a colon at the end of a row or round denote(s) the number of stitches and/or spaces you should have on that row or round.

CROCHET TERMINOLOGY	
UNITED STATES	INTERNATIONAL
slip stitch (slip st) =	single crochet (sc)
single crochet (sc) =	double crochet (dc)
half double crochet (hdc) =	half treble crochet (htr)
double crochet (dc) =	treble crochet(tr)
treble crochet (tr) =	double treble crochet (dtr)
double treble crochet (dtr) =	triple treble crochet (ttr)
triple treble crochet (tr tr) =	quadruple treble crochet (qtr)
skip =	miss

Yarn Weight Symbol & Names	LACE 0	SUPER FINE 1	FINE 2	LIGHT 3	MEDIUM 4	BULKY 5	SUPER BULKY 6
Type of Yarns in Category	Fingering, 10-count crochet thread	Sock, Fingering Baby	Sport, Baby	DK, Light Worsted	Worsted, Afghan, Aran	Chunky, Craft, Rug	Bulky, Roving
Crochet Gauge* Ranges in Single Crochet to 4" (10 cm)	32-42 double crochets**	21-32 sts	16-20 sts	12-17 sts	11-14 sts	8-11 sts	5-9 sts
Advised Hook Size Range	Steel*** 6,7,8 Regular hook B-1	B-1 to E-4	E-4 to 7	7 to I-9	I-9 to K-10.5	K-10.5 to M-13	M-13 and larger

*GUIDELINES ONLY: The chart above reflects the most commonly used gauges and hook sizes for specific yarn categories.

** Lace weight yarns are usually crocheted on larger-size hooks to create lacy openwork patterns. Accordingly, a gauge range is difficult to determine. Always follow the gauge stated in your pattern.

*** Steel crochet hooks are sized differently from regular hooks--the higher the number the smaller the hook, which is the reverse of regular hook sizing.

CROCHET HOOKS															
U.S.	B-1	C-2	D-3	E-4	F-5	G-6	H-8	I-9	J-10	K-10½	L-11	M/N-13	N/P-15	P/Q	Q	S
Metric - mm	2.25	2.75	3.25	3.5	3.75	4	5	5.5	6	6.5	8	9	10	15	16	19

■□□□ BEGINNER	Projects for first-time crocheters using basic stitches. Minimal shaping.
■■□□ EASY	Projects using yarn with basic stitches, repetitive stitch patterns, simple color changes, and simple shaping and finishing.
■■■□ INTERMEDIATE	Projects using a variety of techniques, such as basic lace patterns or color patterns, mid-level shaping and finishing.
■■■■ EXPERIENCED	Projects with intricate stitch patterns, techniques and dimension, such as non-repeating patterns, multi-color techniques, fine threads, small hooks, detailed shaping and refined finishing.

GAUGE (Calibre, muestra)

Exact gauge is **essential** for proper size. Before beginning your Afghan, make the sample swatch given in the individual instructions in the yarn and hook specified. After completing the swatch, measure it, counting your stitches and rows or rounds carefully. If your swatch is larger or smaller than specified, **make another, changing hook size to get the correct gauge.** Keep trying until you find the size hook that will give you the specified gauge.

JOINING WITH SC

When instructed to join with sc, begin with a slip knot on the hook. Insert the hook in the stitch or space indicated, YO and pull up a loop, YO and draw through both loops on hook.

JOINING WITH DC

When instructed to join with a dc, begin with a slip knot on the hook. YO, holding loop on hook, insert the hook in the stitch or space indicated, YO and pull up a loop (3 loops on hook), (YO and draw through 2 loops on hook) twice.

FREE LOOPS OF A CHAIN

When instructed to work in free loops of a beginning ch, work in loop indicated by arrow *(Fig. 3)*.

Fig. 3

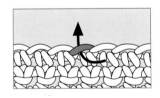

CHANGING COLORS

Work the last stitch to within one step of completion, hook new yarn *(Fig. 4)* and draw through all loops on hook. Cut old yarn and work over both ends.

Fig. 4

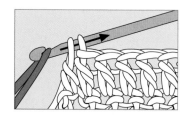

NO SEW JOINING

Hold Strips with **wrong** sides together. Work stitch into space as indicated *(Fig. 5)*.

Fig. 5

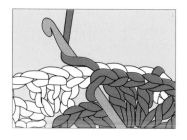

WHIPSTITCH

Place two Strips with **wrong** sides together. Sew through both pieces once to secure the beginning of the seam, leaving an ample yarn end to weave in later. Insert the needle from **front** to **back** through **both** loops of each stitch on **both** pieces *(Fig. 6)*. Bring the needle around and insert it from **front** to **back** through next loops of both pieces. Continue in this manner across, keeping the sewing yarn fairly loose.

Fig. 6

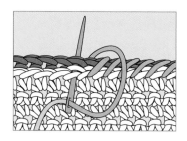

FRINGE

Cut a piece of cardboard 6" (15 cm) wide and ½" (12 mm) longer than you want your finished fringe to be. Wind the yarn **loosely** and **evenly** lengthwise around the cardboard until the card if filled, then cut across one end; repeat as needed.

Hold together as many strands as specified in individual instructions; fold in half.

With **wrong** side facing and using a crochet hook, draw the folded end up through a row and pull the loose ends through the folded end *(Fig. 7a)*; draw the knot up **tightly** *(Fig. 7b)*. Repeat, spacing as specified in individual instructions. Lay Afghan flat on a hard surface and trim the ends.

Fig. 7a

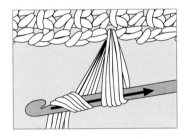

Fig. 7b

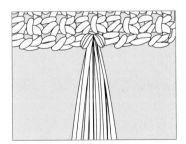

BASIC CROCHET STITCHES

CHAIN

To work a chain stitch, begin with a slip knot on the hook. Bring the yarn **over** the hook from **back** to **front**, catching the yarn with the hook and turning the hook slightly toward you to keep the yarn from slipping off. Draw the yarn through the slip knot *(Fig. 8)* (**first chain st made, abbreviated ch**).

Fig. 8

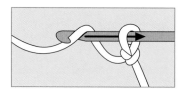

WORKING INTO THE CHAIN

Method 1: Insert the hook into the back ridge of each chain *(Fig. 9a)*.

Fig. 9a

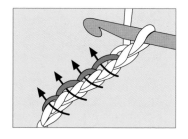

Method 2: Insert the hook under the top two strands of each chain *(Fig. 9b)*.

Fig. 9b

SLIP STITCH

To work a slip stitch, insert the hook in the stitch indicated, YO and draw through the stitch **and** through the loop on hook *(Fig. 10)* **(slip stitch made,** *abbreviated slip st).*

Fig. 10

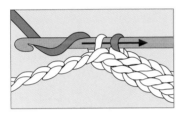

SINGLE CROCHET

Insert the hook in the stitch indicated, YO and pull up a loop, YO and draw through both loops on hook *(Fig. 11)* **(single crochet made,** *abbreviated sc).*

Fig. 11

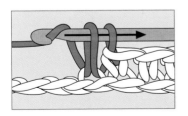

HALF DOUBLE CROCHET

YO, insert the hook in the stitch indicated, YO and pull up a loop, YO and draw through all 3 loops on hook *(Fig. 12)* **(half double crochet made,** *abbreviated hdc).*

Fig. 12

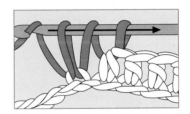

DOUBLE CROCHET

YO, insert the hook in the stitch indicated, YO and pull up a loop (3 loops on hook), YO and draw through 2 loops on hook *(Fig. 13a)*, YO and draw through remaining 2 loops on hook *(Fig. 13b)* **(double crochet made, abbreviated dc)**.

Fig. 13a

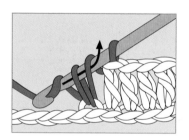

Fig. 13b

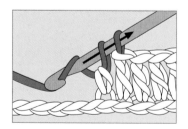

TREBLE CROCHET

YO twice, insert the hook in the stitch indicated, YO and pull up a loop (4 loops on hook) *(Fig. 14a)*, (YO and draw through 2 loops on hook) 3 times *(Fig. 14b)* **(treble crochet made, abbreviated tr)**.

Fig. 14a

Fig. 14b

DOUBLE TREBLE CROCHET

YO 3 times, insert the hook in the stitch indicated, YO and pull up a loop (5 loops on hook) *(Fig. 15a)*, (YO and draw through 2 loops on hook) 4 times *(Fig. 15b)* (**double treble crochet made, abbreviated dtr**).

Fig. 15a

Fig. 15b

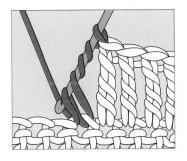
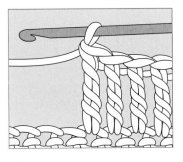

YARN INFORMATION

Each Afghan in this book was made using Light or Medium Weight Yarn. Any brand of Light or Medium Weight Yarn may be used. It is best to refer to the yardage/meters when determining how many balls or skeins to purchase. Remember, to arrive at the finished size, it is the GAUGE/TENSION that is important, not the brand of yarn. Listed below are the specific yarn used to create our photography models.

MILES OF SHELLS
Lion Brand® Vanna's Choice®
Blue - #105 Silver Blue
White - #100 White
Pink - #103 Soft Pink

EASTER MILE-A-MINUTE
Bernat® Softee® Baby
Lavender - #30185 Soft Lilac
Green - #02004 Mint
Yellow - #02003 Lemon

PINEAPPLE PARADE
Bernat® Baby Coordinates
Pink - #48420 Baby Pink
Blue - #48128 Soft Blue

WAVY STRIPS
Red Heart® Soft Baby®
Green - #7624 Lime
Lavender - #7588 Lilac
White - #7001 White

LEMON DROP
Red Heart® Baby Love™
White - #1001 Milk
Yellow - #0210 Banana

DAISIES FOR BABY
Bernat® Softee® Baby
White - #02000 White
Yellow - #02003 Lemon
Green - #02004 Mint

Production Team: Writer/Instructional Editor - Sarah J. Green; Editorial Writer - Susan Frantz Wiles; Graphic Artist - Becca Snider Tally; Senior Graphic Artist - Lora Puls.

We have made every effort to ensure that these instructions are accurate and complete. We cannot, however, be responsible for human error, typographical mistakes, or variations in individual work.